MW00412494

STREET STORIES

RICK REYNOLDS

Designed by Blake Quackenbush and Eleni Hannula
Compiled by University Communications
Seattle Pacific University
3307 Third Avenue West
Seattle, WA 98119
ISBN-13: 978-1506104324
ISBN-10: 1506104320

Operation Nightwatch
P.O. Box 21181
Seattle, WA 98111

seattlenightwatch.org

CONTENTS

2004

2005

2006

2007

2008

2009

CONTENTS

2011

2012

2013

CONTENTS

2014

LUKE RUTAN

RICK REYNOLDS

Foreward

One of the most comfort-zone-extending experiences of my 42 years of pastoral ministry was putting on a clerical collar and walking the nighttime streets of Seattle under Rick Reynolds' guidance. Rick — an urban minister par excellence — taught me and other street ministers to express unconditional respect and care for the downtown homeless and for troubled patrons of bars seeking conversation.

Rick is at home with city leaders, up-scale urbanites, and the homeless of Seattle. He has a huge heart of compassion for the troubled men and women of our city, and especially for the urban poor. Many of their gripping stories are included in this book's collection of Rick's blog posts.

Although he tries to redirect attention and honor to others who serve and support the work of Operation Nightwatch, he has become its face in our city. It would be hard to imagine Operation Nightwatch without the smiling, caring person at its head, Rick Reynolds.

Rick has been anchored in the church community where I was pastor for many years. He teaches adult classes, works with youth, serves Communion, helps with church dinners, and was one of the best-received guest speakers in our church, as well as in many other area congregations.

I join with his friends, co-workers, and supporters in honoring Rick Reynolds, executive director of Operation Nightwatch and urban minister par excellence. Rick lives out the words of Jesus: "As much as you do it to the least of these, you do it to me."

H. Mark Abbott, Pastor Emeritus
First Free Methodist Church
Seattle, Washington

2004

04 THURSDAY JULY 29

Hot Night on the Street

Okay, it's all relative. Seattle is hot at 80 degrees. It is the end of the month, more homeless people show up at the shelters. People are cranky.

So tonight one of our local politicians, Seattle City Councilperson Tom Rasmussen took a tour of my world. What a guy!

Here's what he saw:

Volunteers at Nightwatch heating soup and setting out sandwiches.

A homeless family: Dad, mom (pregnant), and preschool kid, getting sent off to a cheap hotel room, and getting some good counsel on what to do tomorrow to get longer-term help.

First Avenue Service Center, where the crew was mopping the floor and getting ready for the onslaught of homeless guys.

St. Martin de Porres shelter, where 200+ older men reside.

We got back to the Operation Nightwatch dispatch center, where homeless men and women were waiting to go out to shelter someplace around Seattle. The heat caused tempers to flare. Words exchanged, staff intervened. No punches thrown, thank God.

It's just too darn hot tonight.

04 WEDNESDAY AUGUST 04

First Fight

I was driving up Jackson Street today, and saw "Ralph" making a deal at a bus stop. He's still alive after ten years, which is something of a miracle.

Here's how we first met.

It was my third day on the job as director of Operation Nightwatch. I was sitting at a desk in our little storefront located at First and Wall in Belltown, just a few blocks north of the Pike Place Market in Seattle.

Suddenly I heard the sounds of a fight right outside my glass front door. Ralph, who is small, wiry, and African-American, is swapping punches with some tall white guy, right in our entry.

This was something new for me, white-bread suburban boy. Emergency! Emergency!

I ran over to the phone and called 911.

"There's a fight, two guys going at it, 2415 First Ave!" I am shaking and breathless talking to the dispatcher.

"Is anyone hurt?" she asked. I looked outside again. Ralph and the other guy are still on their feet taking big wild swings and occasionally landing one.

"I guess not, they're still on their feet."

"Are there any weapons?" she asked. I looked again.

"Just fists," I told her.

"Then call us back." Click. →

I decided I was going to have to do something myself. So I went out onto the sidewalk. Here were the two fighters on the ground next to the curb. By this time Ralph was sitting on the bigger white guy's chest, popping him in the cheek with his fist, but not that hard.

Leaning over them both, I said loudly, "HEY, KNOCK IT OFF!" Ralph looked up at me, standing over him in a clerical collar (you know I'm a minister, right?), and he immediately jumps off the guy.

The two combatants are surrounded by their friends. The "loser" staggers away with two buddies consoling him. Everyone around Ralph was patting him on the back. "Way to go, that guy was drunk, he was picking fights with everyone, whatta pain in the neck."

I thought to myself. Here was a drunk white guy picking a fight with a bunch of homeless guys, and if the police had come they would have seen Ralph sitting on the guy's chest trying to sober him up, sorta. Then they would have arrested the wrong guy. So I figured it all worked out for the best.

04 SUNDAY AUGUST 08

Guy in the Alley

Some guy was lying down in the alley. Not that unusual for homeless person, you're thinking? Yeah, but this guy was in the very middle of the alley, smell of piss permeating the air. The city would send a street cleaner through several times a week, blowing sudsy water around. It didn't help.

So here was some guy in the stinky alley, in the middle of the day. I was going to have to step over him

"Hey, are you all right?"

He opened one eye, lifted his head. "I'm good." But I could see a string of melted gum sticking to the back of his head.

It seems like such a good idea to get homeless people to tell us what they need. But like many people, homeless or not homeless, we don't always know what we need.

04 SATURDAY AUGUST 21

Out of Control

I walked into a bar on Wednesday night and immediately some woman covered her face. Why? I don't know. (Maybe I just have that effect on people.)

Her friend cut in on her, started talking my ear off — angry, beat up by life. She's Navaho, had a bad family experience. She trotted out her spiritual pedigree — it's one of the most common reactions to seeing a minister in a bar. I'll sit down, and immediately some guy will say, "I used to be an altar boy, thought about being a priest, grandma took me to Sunday school, I went to Catholic grade school," etc., etc., etc.

My Navaho friend talked about sage grass, and visions, and other Navaho practices. But this was no exchange or conversation. She was angry at life, angry at me, just angry. I let her run with it. I did not say a word. Finally, she ran down, and asked me what I thought about it all. "I'm just here to listen."

She was amazed. That was the last answer she thought she would get. She wandered off to another patron.

Now I could turn my attention to her friend, the woman who covered her face when I walked into the bar.

She, too, shared some of the pain of her life — homeless, separated from loved ones. But at the heart of her sorrow was remorse and repentance. We had only a few moments together, but as I was leaving she asked for me to pray for her.

I put my hand on her, and said a prayer, but I used her street handle "Coyote." She quietly interrupted. "Use my Christian name." So I blessed her and sought God's help for her, using her "real" name.

04 WEDNESDAY AUGUST 25

"Ronnie" Kisses Me

"Ronnie" was about the homeliest, smelliest, loudest homeless guy at Nightwatch in our Shelter Dispatch Program. Every night he'd come in, juiced up and mouthing off. The shelters wouldn't take him from us anymore because of his wild behavior. He seemed incapable of controlling himself. I'm sure he was used to having people yell at him daily, so I started whispering.

"Ronnie, you can't talk that way here," I would tell him, and he would whisper back, "Okay!"

One memorable night we had conned some new shelter worker into taking Ronnie off our hands. He was standing in the middle of a room full of homeless guys with his pass into a shelter, and a big crooked grin on his face.

"Pastor Rick, ain't I beautiful?" he asked me.

I realized that every person in that room was waiting to see if I was going to lie. I didn't disappoint.

"Sure, Ronnie, you're beautiful." Yeah, he's in the image of God, right?

"Then hug me."

I recoiled inwardly, not wanting to get close this smelly guy. I tried to get next to him to give him one of those friendly used-car-salesman hugs around one shoulder, but he turned toward me and threw his arms around me in a huge bear hug, his 6'2" bending down over me, his rough cheek pressed against mine, the smell of cheap booze and smoke and BO wafting over me.

Then he kissed me on the cheek and went off into the night. It was a God moment. →

I was patting myself on the back about the good thing I had done, until a little nagging voice asked me a question.

"Who was being the ugly one in that situation?" I realized that I had wanted to keep Ronnie at arm's length, keep him away from me. He, on the other hand, threw his arms around me with glorious exuberant joy. I was the one who was being ugly.

Help me love everyone with Your uninhibited joy!

04 MONDAY AUGUST 30

Don't Want to Be Here

My good friend Dick Shipe was hit and killed on the way to work. I did NOT want to be riding herd on a bunch of knuckleheads at Operation Nightwatch twelve hours later. I needed time with family and friends, time to reflect on a lost friendship.

About 10:00 p.m. I was fed up to here.

I marched out on the sidewalk and stuck my finger in the face of some galoot named, ironically, Richard.

"What makes you do this every night?" I asked him, my sorrow and anger boiling over. This guy was smart, street savvy, and aggressive. At least with the little guys.

Richard pulled me away from his friends about fifteen feet. "Pastor Rick, I'm dying of testicular cancer, and I want to die a man, on the street."

Suddenly I realized that we were co-travelers through the pains of life; he was grieving, I was grieving.

I apologized for embarrassing him in front of his friends, and told him about the death of my friend.

Richard laid his hands on my shoulders and said, "Pastor Rick, I'm going to say a prayer for you." He prayed for my comfort, the comfort of the family who lost a loved one, the tenderest of prayers.

04 MONDAY OCTOBER 18

BIG, BIG Family

This place can take your breath away.

Because we were hosting a new group, and because I ended up cooking for them, and because they are friends of mine, I was hanging out on a Saturday night. I thought maybe just once I would be able to get the people started and get out of here at a decent time.

But then the hurricane arrived in the form of a rather large family:

- Mom, age 33
- Stepdad, age 26
- 17-year-old daughter
- Her 2-week-old daughter
- The father of the baby
- 14-year-old daughter
- 12-year-old son
- 11-year-old son
- 9-year-old son
- 8-year-old son
- 6-year-old son
- 5-year-old daughter
- 3-year-old daughter

They arrived this weekend in a minivan, driving from Louisiana. At age thirty-three, the mother had her first baby at thirteen. They drove straight through in three days. I'm not even sure that's possible, and especially with all those kids and sleeping in the van in rest stops on the way here. But the seventeen-year-old daughter who is a mother said it only took them three days, two nights.'

We got them settled in a cheap hotel for a few nights, gave them a list of resources. We filled their tank with gas (the father dodged into the quickie-mart and got a job app!). I don't know how they physically survived. I put four of the kids into my car for the run to the hotel, and still their van was crowded. They made quite an impression; half of them were bare footed when they got into the dispatch center.

What are they thinking? And more importantly, where will they go today?

04 THURSDAY DECEMBER 02

Drunk AND Cranky

Every night is different.

About the time I think I've seen it all in twenty years of going out on the street, then something new and weird happens.

Thursday night Father Kim and I were making our usual rounds. We were having a good time with the regulars at one of our favorite stops. (I can't say where we were this time; we're going back there next week and I don't want more guff from anyone.)

Anyway, "George" was really drunk, sitting two barstools away from me. I'm having a nice conversation with Cat Lady about public housing.

Almost every interaction I have with George has been unhappy — he's always working too hard trying to figure out what we're doing there, and he's angry with the world anyway, so the anger gets directed to me. I tend just to tune him out because he's talking BLEEP and being totally inappropriate. Probably needs to be cut off, but the owner/bartender is over-serving everyone anyway — how a drunk can decide when another drunk has had enough is beyond me.

So I'm having this nice conversation and George starts in on me about why I'm not out saving homeless people — ordering me to go to City Hall Park where all the homeless people hang at night, putting us down for hanging out for an hour at his bar, getting really loud.

I had enough. I told him we go to his bar because that's where the people who end up at City Hall Park start out their drinking careers. As to wasting our time, I asked him why he wasn't out selling real estate, since that's what he does for a living. He shut up for a while.

Then he came over and talked with Father Kim. “I like his church, I don’t like yours,” he stated. I said it’s okay, because he goes to both our churches equally, meaning never. Then he gave a big sloppy drunken hug to Father Kim.

When we left Father Kim quietly observed that the guy was mad at himself for not dealing with his drinking. If we can irritate him enough, maybe something will change. I’ll keep bugging him.

04 WEDNESDAY DECEMBER 08

Drug Dealer

Okay, so it's been awhile since I've had such a long talk with a dealer. I'm still not sure what I think about this one.

I'm sitting at one of Seattle's finest second-class dives talking to a homeless friend. A young woman (okay, she fessed to being forty) greeted my friend, and bummed some tobacco, and stood talking to us both.

"I only sell marijuana," she said. Well, she was drinking an Olde English 800 Malt Liquor (about double the alcohol of a typical strong beer) so maybe she has other interests?

Wonder what her life is like? She sleeps in her car except when she swaps bud for a couch with a "friend." She has lived for a year on the street.

Why just marijuana? "I saw cocaine and heroin when I was ten; I saw what it did to people and how evil it made them."

She pauses to greet two customers. Or maybe they were her suppliers.

After Brother Dave and I left the bar, he told me the bar employee was still using horse.

About 1:30 in the morning I wondered if she was the young woman (same name) who came to my church in the late 1970s (about the right age), located on Capitol Hill (the neighborhood she identified as her childhood place). Add thirty years and fifty pounds. Could it be?

2005

05 SUNDAY FEBRUARY 20

My Alien Encounter

He wanted instructions to the bus tunnel — but we were on First Hill in Seattle, a long confusing walk for someone with bad English skills. Since I wasn't going to get home anytime soon anyway I offered to drop him off by one of the tunnel entrances.

On the way downtown I found out his name "Benigno." He is Portuguese, and has been here for over a year on a tourist visa. For most of the past twelve months he worked day labor jobs using a phony social security number. His employer caught up with him at the end of the year and reluctantly let him go.

How does someone survive without being able to work a regular job?

For now Benigno is sleeping in a camper/van loaned to him by someone in Tukwila. He is applying for hotel/casino work. He has high hopes, since he met another illegal Portuguese person working at such a place.

Later in the week we met so I could show him around town. Shelter, day program, work program. He is fluent in all the Latin languages. He is young and personable and clean-cut.

He came to the U.S. naively believing he would be able to earn enough money to buy a house back home. Now he's stuck.

Do you think you know what homelessness is all about?

When we debate immigration policy, we have to figure out what to do with the Benignos once they're here, doing jobs most Americans don't want.

05 WEDNESDAY APRIL 06

Eastmont Wildcats!

Sunday night I took about thirty kids from Wenatchee, Washington, out on the street to give them an education about Seattle and homelessness.

We started from the crest of Yesler Hill, just above I-5. A greenbelt extends from Yesler to James Street, homeless trails going the length of it, with camping areas under young evergreens. The area is bordered by public housing, and the parking building for Harborview Hospital.

We walked toward the waterfront, trying to imagine the old growth timber, which would be shoved down to the waterfront along this route (the origin of "Skid Road"). At the bottom of the hill we could see City Hall Park at Third and Yesler, where a feeding program was just wrapping up.

"Where you guys from?" one of the meal patrons asked.

"I'm from Operation Nightwatch, and I'm taking this group of kids from Wenatchee out on a tour."

"I graduated from Eastmont High in Wenatchee."

Now what are the odds of that? I take a group of kids out from a small town three hours away, and the first homeless guy we run into is from their school.

05 WEDNESDAY MAY 25

"Michael" in the Hood

Okay, so the Messiah turns out to live in the hood. I didn't know it.

He walked into the dispatch center last year — in the fall. Anyway "Michael" had shown up in our shelter dispatch program at 11:30 p.m. — an old lady in tow. We managed to get this grandma a place in one of the women's shelters for the night, while Michael pulled me aside to tell me he was the Messiah. I told him I thought what he meant was that he was a disciple. I encouraged him to come back during the day to visit me so we could talk some more about it.

I never heard from him until about three weeks ago.

He started showing up again — he lives in an assisted-living program nearby. We've been having these charming talks the past few weeks — I try to cut through the mental illness stuff — and focus on reassuring him that he is loved, that he's not beyond hope. He wanted me to hear his confession of all his sin — going steadily forward from age four (stabbing a sibling with a pencil) to recent bad choices. Now I'm trying to get him to identify small steps he can take to help others, and live in the realization of being forgiven.

Mental illness and religion — requirement or impediment? Kidding.

So, now we're on a schedule — 4:00 Thursday our thirty minutes together. It is manageable, and it keeps me on my toes. Pray for us.

05 SATURDAY JUNE 18

Strange Apostle's Creed

So twenty years on the street and I never had this one happen before.

I'm in one of my regular haunts. Drunk/high person, "Pssst. You help me, I help you. I can tell you selling drugs people."

What?

"You want to know who selling?"

I don't care. You think I'm a cop? I don't care.

He wasn't paying any attention. I finally had to get away from him pestering me. Another guy comes up to me and shows me his Catholic tattoo. "Hey, Father."

"No, I'm Methodist." (The short answer).

Well, I'm Catholic, and here's what I believe:

"I believe in God the Father, maker of heaven and earth ...," and the dude rattles off the entire Apostles' Creed, me reciting right with him.

"Holy Catholic church ..." He was surprised I said that part of the creed (catholic, little c; means universal. He actually knew that. It was news to him that Methodists could agree on that). The next thing he said, "I don't really think it matters what church — but Jesus Christ died for my sins."

Right on. We parted friends.

05 FRIDAY JULY 29

Somali Family

Came in to a mess tonight. A homeless Somali family with five kids, one more on the way. I stuffed them into my Subaru (thank God — no crash and no police) and took them to a north Seattle hotel.

Now, usually Operation Nightwatch can only pay for one night, and on occasions — like a weekend — we will pay for two. It isn't much time to figure out next steps. But I approved four nights, which will get the family through Sunday night. Partly I could do this because the hotel agreed to put seven people in a regular room (two kings) for a reasonable cost.

We pulled into the hotel parking lot and poured out of the car. The kids each took a share of the baggage and grocery sacks, I carried the three-year-old boy who had fallen asleep in the twenty-minute car ride from downtown. The wife said something to the husband who translated. "She say, 'Whatever you want in the next life, God should give you.'" I thanked her.

Now the hotel clerk saw this huge family and took it all in stride. The sign-in procedure was accomplished, and then the most amazing thing happened. It isn't the fanciest hotel in the world — lots of poor folk getting by here. So we went to the room, and the clerk actually helped to carry the baggage, just like the best hotel in the world. It was truly amazing and heartwarming.

As we said our goodbyes, the wife had one more really nice thing to say to me. She had a large heavy duty plastic shopping bag with her. "This bag was given to me by a European in the refugee camp in Kenya. I keep it with me and I never will forget that person who gave it to me. And I will never forget you either."

I think she'll name the baby after me.

05 FRIDAY SEPTEMBER 02

Another Great Quote

Father Kim was out of town so I was on my own last night.

Had several people invoke my clergy privilege last night — so I can't really share any of the big news from my favorite Queen Anne bar. Needless to say it will affect us all; these sorts of events can cause people to seek personal change and growth — painful, but ultimately good.

Had a great visit at Third and Bell, although I've got tell you, there was a ton of street drug trafficking going on. All these twitchy people gathering, then suddenly dispersing, and looking at me in a most paranoid fashion.

At Third and Bell saw several regulars, though R#3 was AWOL. I think he should have to call us if he's NOT going to be there. I don't think he drinks, just likes the company. Anyway, D. was thankful I was attempting to assist him. Not sure if there's anything we can do, his name and birth certificate don't match — his service record, etc., all with a name he wasn't born with. But I suspect after talking with him — if he had the identification at some point, he can get it again, assuming he's accurate in his info. We shall see. He's sixty-five and sleeps outside and believes he shouldn't anymore. The last few times I've seen him a little sloppier than I remember in times past, not sure what to make of it other than the usual progression of the disease.

Some guy started chatting me up in the bathroom (hard to describe it as a bathroom, the door is stuck open and the back of your head is clearly visible to the bartender — in fact when I first went in there last night, she stopped me, turned me around for a hug — her in the door of the men's room and me inside. HA.

Anyway, a guy followed me in, and started talking over his shoulder (any guy can explain this if you ask them). Anyway, he said something like how important it is to do good, and I tried to shape this thought a →

little — because I believe it is biblical that we are "blessed to be a blessing." It wasn't exactly what he meant (probably more like "what goes around comes around" or that misunderstood idea of making good karma for oneself). Anyway we had this little patch of common ground, and I went back out to the bar to my interrupted conversation. Suddenly this hand was thrust into mine with some real folding money. I was sort of mid thought and didn't really look at what was handed me, and when I finished my sentence, turned around, and the dude was gone.

The other patrons thought it was pretty cool that he had done that but when I said something about sending the money to help people in New Orleans, they vetoed it. "It's for Nightwatch," so there you go.

Plus another great quote: "My mother was Lutheran and my dad was Roman Catholic. I'm a Little Schizophrenic."

05 FRIDAY OCTOBER 14

Dreamy Night

Did you ever have one of those dreams where people you knew from here, there, and everywhere intruded into your brain. It was like that last night at Third and Bell.

Pastor Dave and I returned to the Dravus Street bar looking for evacuees from My Favorite (closed) Queen Anne tavern. Did not spot anyone, but greeted "Bartender C," who seems completely out of context in a pretty rough bar — she should be pushing milk and cheese products at a country fair, dressed in dirndl skirt.

Pastor Dave whipped me at pool (lousy table) and then beat one guy, lost to another. He wanted me to think he threw the game for the sake of the gospel!

Then I entered a twilight zone. Six significant conversations at Third and Bell — people wandering in that I knew ten years ago, former homeless people I helped out (arguing about who has known me longer). One meth babe who confessed to being a grandmother (I was watching the face of the thirty-year-old who HAD been hitting on her — hehehehe — sin is often its own reward). The Man With No Identity received my letter to the senator on his behalf. Tree Hugger K walked in carrying a gallon of milk (what the!!!) and let me know that he isn't drinking anymore (or did he say, "not drinking very much?"). At any rate, he walked out of Third and Bell with his milk and never had a drop o' booze despite hanging out and talking. The thirty-year-old "kid" who had hit on the meth-babe-granny was full of himself; moved out of Belltown ("I don't have to throw macaroni and cheese out my window onto drug dealers now." — best quote of the night) and lives in Magnolia neighborhood. Good for him. He was pretty stoked.

New bartender — I'll call him Second Gospel — is settling in. ➞

I can't remember laughing so much on the street in twenty years.

Oh, yeah, how could I forget. Bearded Lutheran told me he's now been on the same stretch of I-5 for fifteen years (which is consistent with the fact that I first met him ten years ago and at that time he told me it was five years. He inspired me back then to clamber under the freeway to meet people.)

We had a wide-ranging conversation — military service and the directions of a person's life given certain pivotal moments and choices we make. Serious stuff. He grew up Missouri Synod Lutheran. Interesting guy. About twenty minutes into this wide-ranging conversation, he pulls up and says, "Pray for {me}," saying his full name. Nothing specific. I assured him I would, and he said, "I believe you will." It was quite a serious moment in a night of hilarity.

05 FRIDAY OCTOBER 21

Do-It-Yourself WHAT?

Another unbelievable night.

Started by running four cases of blankets to Seattle's Tent City 3 — we heard they were low. There was a total screaming fracas going on at the leadership tent, some woman was yelling in a voice that would fracture cement. Decided to drop and run.

Off to our new Dravus Street bar — Milk Maid bartender, always seems out of context to me in this rough, tough place. But she likes seeing us, anxious to talk.

A Lumberjack — big guy in plaid and bad teeth picks up on my church affiliation — Free Methodist. He has a story to tell.

He grew up Free Methodist, married a Jewish woman. Their son's Jewish, but his wife isn't observant. He "cleans up," because she wants the Christmas tree and he wants the menorah and Hanukah in the house.

After his son was born, the Jewish grandmother wants to know who will do the bris (the ritual circumcision)?

Lumberjack looks me right in the face. "I did it myself, I told her. And it's the truth." No, Lumberjack is no mohel. His physician buddy had done the work, while he said the words of the Covenant over his son.

Hey, it counts.

Onto Third and Bell, need to find a wheelchair for R#3 — his bearing went out. He can still get around with a cane, but when he's tired, it's a bit dicey. And I've noticed he's AWOL more often lately (remember, he only drinks coffee).

Second Gospel bartending tonight. Knew my name. Sheesh.

05 TUESDAY NOVEMBER 15

Man Has Identity Restored!

The "Man With No Identity" needs a new blog name, since today, the unbelievable happened.

This saga goes back about four months. In my efforts to get MWNI off the street, all these obstacles emerged — wallet stolen (everything missing). Name on his birth certificate different than the name he used in the military. Almost thirty years since he had a Washington state driver's license. No way to collect Social Security, despite his being sixty-five years old.

We got his service record from the military, and with that, just today, got into the federal building (without ID — sorta catch-22); they escorted us upstairs and within fifteen minutes we walked out with official VA ID card, complete with picture, signature, date of birth. Yee-Haw.

Walking up second Ave. in downtown Seattle, it was surreal. "I am somebody," he said.

"Since we're on a roll, let's go get you a Washington state ID card," I suggested. He resisted. No way. They're never going to give me that, I tried before." C'mon, let us try anyway, see what happens.

Thirty minutes later we had his temporary Washington state ID, the permanent one comes in three weeks. Unreal. MWNI is now the Man With Identity. Thanks to those who prayed: Luther Memorial Men's Group, Mistie, Dan, Gerard, Jim, and others.

05 MONDAY NOVEMBER 28

Thanksgiving

I decided to go out to visit my bars on Thanksgiving night. This is the first time in twenty years I've actually tried this, partly to preserve my own sanity and partly to keep the home fires burning. But last week I checked and, yes, both the main bars I go to were planning to be open. What do you expect? People to suddenly have a life? Besides, by 10:00 p.m. on a holiday a lot of people feel like going out and getting drunk — thanks to family tension.

The Dravus Street bar was open — some recognizable regulars — though I haven't seen "J" for awhile, and Dogboy was AWOL. I miss the lumber-jack/mohel. Milk Maid behind the bar described her cooking calamity — turkey avalanche when the entire oven tipped forward and dropped a bunch of equipment on her, to say nothing of a 350-degree bird. She's gonna be sore tomorrow.

Down the bar was a lone guy working on a pitcher. He offered to buy me a beer. I demurred, but came down and sat with him and had a reasonably lucid conversation (one of these days I'm going to lay out a system for categorizing bar conversations — instead of one to five stars they would have to be one to five pint glasses ...). This RC patron talked about a family situation. He also had some nice things to say about Nightwatch from years gone by — apparently he bartended in the area when there were more ministers on the street. God bless him, I was really happy to have had one "one pint" type conversation. Made coming out to night worth it.

Went on down to Third and Bell. "K" says he had a fine meal — cooked himself dinner, ate alone. I gave the "Man With No ID" his new driver's license, which arrived this week. He is really ready to move in someplace, hopefully here at Nightwatch. Lots of women from Angelines hanging out — evidently they come to the bar to wait for their rides to various shelters. Lots of Hispanic guys in tonight. "R"#3 was gone still. ➛

Third Gospel in the bar, looking good. Don't see button down shirts often back there. Silent "M" enjoyed the conversation — some sort of affective disorder — stroke or something. Another vet.

Back at Nightwatch — a wild man was talking to the martians, but the crew wasn't concerned about him. They deal with him nightly and he doesn't seem to pose a threat to anyone. What a life. In early (midnight home).

05 THURSDAY DECEMBER 01

MFQAB Reopens!!

Yeah! My Favorite Queen Anne Bar has reopened. Under new management and looking unbelievable. Met the new owner (we try not to use real names of establishments or people). Definitely a different type place, very nice, very nonsmoky. In fact there were more people clustered outside than inside drinking. It will be interesting when this nonsmoking rule goes into effect.

But I'm getting ahead of myself on a busy night. It's really cold tonight, but early in the month many people have checks and go rent cheap rooms in hotels, or just plain party all night. So there's excess shelter space, though there is snow on the ground.

First stop after checking in at Nightwatch (Fourteenth and Main) was to Harborview Hospital. Here we visited our ailing tenant. He's pretty out of it. Started to say, "Don't take any ..." one would presume "wooden nickels" but he fumbled a bit, then said, " "Don't take any hookers." When I asked him what he meant, he just laughed and said, "You know what I mean, right there, you know?" All I could do is think, "huh?"

From Harborview we scooted down to the Dravus Street Bar. Always interesting. Had a cup of java, greeted the Milk Maid Bartender, and regulars: "H," "J," "K." H is driving me crazy because I can never remember if he's Harry or Howard or Homer or Horton, and I've met him too often to not remember. Alzheimers? If I remember properly how to spell it I must not be suffering. Oh, and note to self: The crazy kid is not Dogboy — misinformed. He's Goulet.

Here's a replay of my "conversation" with Goulet. He asks me an unintelligible theological question, then takes umbrage at my response of "excuse me?" Then he tells me, "A lot of people touched the Bible before anyone ever read it." Ah, I think, a discussion of textual criticism and →

documentary reliability. Before I can respond he asks me if I have ever asked God about aliens controlling humans with microwave energy so that we will fight with each other. He got up and moved, and I pondered the likelihood of alcohol psychosis.

As we were leaving (we, being Father Kim and I) we were stopped by one honest man — a Scotch-Irish "I" (Hey, he fits in very well with the list of regulars above!). Grew up agnostic acknowledged his lost-ness. His blunt openness was refreshing. Hope we run into I again.

Milk Maid came all the way out to the sidewalk to thank us. (She was afraid we wouldn't come back after MFQAB reopens — we started going to her joint looking for MFQAB evacuees two or three months ago.

Anyway, from Milk Maid to the yuppiefied but nice MFQAB. Kind of quiet, hasn't had its grand reopening yet. After being empty for three months, it will take time for word to get out. But it was good to see some regulars, they seemed happy to see us. The whole place is muted and rich in feel, very different but cool. And NO SMOKING.

On down to Third and Bell. Place was packed — first of the month, people have dough in welfare land. Third Gospel looking natty in the bar, R#3 playing pool and looking as healthy as I've ever seen him, sans wheelchair. "K" greeted us warmly as usual, and the Man With No Identity there as usual. I need another name for him, now that he's got two pieces of picture ID and is soon going to get Social Security. Hope the room opens for him in our building.

We had a deeper conversation than usual — me trying to fit a wedge between the Catholic priest who got in the worst bar fight he's ever seen, and a living love faith relationship with the Creator. Every human being is broken and at some level a failure. This does not negate the fact that

God can use them for a good purpose. We all sin. But God loves us. I think MWNI is getting it. I also took the opportunity to pick at the source of some of his anger with family over money and respect. He wished me a happy Christmas, but I pointed out I would see him at least three more times before Christmas.

Home to Nightwatch — where there was a quiet night, no turn-aways and no problems. Off to bed!

2006

06 WEDNESDAY APRIL 19

Resurrection

Maybe because it's the week after Easter (at least for Western Christianity) I thought about resurrections I have witnessed. Walt is one.

He was drunk when I met him in line outside Operation Nightwatch, but he said something no homeless guy had ever said to me in twenty-plus years on the street: "Pastor Rick, I've determined that never again in my life will I own a lawn mower."

The next day he stopped by my office, and I invited him to move into our building as a tenant. This led to three months of hell.

Now, if you have never seen someone toxic from alcohol, it is not a pretty sight. Walt proceeded to get drunk every day, blowing out effluvia from both ends. I found him wandering the halls of the apartment building draped in a towel, covered with BM from his head to his feet. And the smell cannot be described. We determined to clean out his room while he was in the hospital. (He gave his drunken permission when the fire department hauled him away.) The load of excrement and carpet/furniture/mattress was so bad that I had tears in my eyes, tying down the tarp along the side of a windy freeway. Okay, enough grossness.

What happened next is also beyond description, a total God-thing. Walt fell and broke his back.

He went off to Swedish Hospital, spent thirty days in traction and detoxed at the same time. He came back to a different unit in our building, a changed man. That was six years ago.

I had not heard from Walt in a few months (he had moved from our building into several different great places), and I was getting worried. I called his last housemate and his workplace to see if he was still okay.

So last night, Father Kim and I started our night on the street with a visit to Walt's place in Ballard.

He looked amazing, and his apartment is really stylish. Hard to believe it's the same guy. He's working, keeping really busy with driving for a food bank, volunteering for Homeland Security duties with the Coast Guard Auxiliary, an ambassador at the Woodland Park Zoo, and other interests.

When I am in a church that recites the Apostles' Creed and get to "I believe in ... the resurrection of the body," I always will think of the resurrection of Walt.

Once you get a taste of that, you want more!

06 FRIDAY APRIL 21

April 21st Birthday

This day, April 21st, never goes by without my remembering my friend Ron.

We were just a month apart in age, good friends growing up. When Ron was in ninth grade, he started exhibiting signs of schizophrenia. By the time I was in college, he was in and out of institutions, often times on the street, or living in a halfway house, or a commune someplace. Then in 1976, he disappeared, never to be seen again in Seattle.

For years his absence haunted me. Then one night I had a dream. Ron knocked on my front door and said, "Look! I'm fine!"

I took it to mean he was in the presence of God, and I haven't worried since.

But every once in a while I look at some homeless guy at Operation Nightwatch and wonder, what would Ron look like now, on his fifty-third birthday? Behold, God is our salvation, I shall trust, and not be afraid ...

P.S., Ron's parents volunteer for Operation Nightwatch.

Tribute to a Friend

We were best friends when we were little.
I stayed overnight at your house.
You stayed overnight at mine.
But thirty years ago you began hearing
What no one else could hear.
You saw things no one could see.
Then you disappeared down the highway,
Seeking relief from a tortured mind.

In my heart, I believe you arrived
At a place of rest and peace;
And I think you landed there quietly.

But I still see you in dreams,
And I still look carefully at each face.
I'm not the only one looking.
I'm not the only one remembering.
I'm not the only one with a loved one
on the street.

06 MONDAY APRIL 24

Church to the Rescue

I was downtown for a meeting, dodged into Third and Bell (weird to see one of these in the daytime). Second Gospel behind the bar, like usual, and some of the usual regulars in the middle of the afternoon. Someone I knew had to use the doorless toilet.

Standing there, suddenly R#2 (can't use his real name, in fact, I'm not even going to use his street name because everyone will know who I mean), grabbed me and hauled me out onto the sidewalk.

"I went crazy, went to see my daughter, don't have money for rent." He waved a letter from his landlord showing how much he owed. It wasn't much, just over $200. "One of the churches is going to help some."

Now, I thought about it. This guy is a pretty good guy, kooky, but good hearted. He wants to help homeless people. Do we really want him coming to the Nightwatch shelter dispatch for a mat on the floor somewhere?

I gave him my card. "Call me, we can probably do something."

The next day, the pastor of the church called me. This is the second time in two months R#2 has needed help. Different reasons every time. The pastor is not going to walk away, however. They're going to help R#2 with what he really needs — some protective payee care, along with the check. The church agreed to help with the full amount. Wow. They think someone is preying on R#2. Could be. Thank God for faithful congregations and pastors.

06 THURSDAY APRIL 27

My Helper

So now when I go out to speak I'm taking a neighbor with me — my friend the Messiah (kind of a mean nick name now that he knows better — but that is how he introduced himself to me eighteen months ago).

It really does help me to have the Messiah with me when I go talk. He adds an edge to what I talk about related to homelessness (he's not homeless, but a little obsessive about it — not sure what his diagnosis is, but suffice to say he's out there). Plus, he is an extra set of hands for carrying stuff. He has always been very appropriate too, which is nice. Maybe I'll see if he wants his pic in the blog sometime.

So yesterday we were at a class at Seattle Pacific University (spu.edu) and the teacher, very cool — Delia Nuesch Olver — interviewed me, and students asked questions, and the ninety minutes flew by. It feels a little constraining, but she wants to keep me in check — it isn't a fund-raising effort. They actually need to learn something.

06 FRIDAY SEPTEMBER 01

Believe It or Not

"You're Methodist? My family was Methodist."

I started feeling a little scritchy in the back of my brain, wondering where we were going with this.

It's the seediest bar around, Bob Marley wailing in the background, lots of whispers and coming and going. The guy is lit up but not too bad.

"I don't really ... well, I guess I do believe that stuff. Well, some of it anyway," he faltered.

I recognized in the faltering that he wasn't really going to deny his faith — the faltering meant there was something still there that said, "I can't prove I believe anything, but to say that I don't believe is worrisome, and if it is worrisome, I must believe, something at least."

The next words he said to me nailed it: "I'm too old for this."

"For what?"

"All this — propositioned, offered drugs. I've got a ten-year-old," and then silence as he thought about how many beers and how long he was sitting in darkness with a bunch of thugs.

"Nice to meet you." He shook my hand and headed out. It was 10:00 p.m. He left two-thirds of a beer on the counter.

06 TUESDAY OCTOBER 03

Little Things Matter

I really don't like wearing neckties; wearing a clerical collar is not much relief. Each new clerical shirt comes with a pair of plastic tabs, the little white square that makes that distinctive look for the ministers on the street.

When I pull out that tab and unbutton my minister's shirt, it looks rather ordinary. Pop the little white tab back in, and voila — street minister/chaplain/priest.

Those little plastic strips keep disappearing on me. They turn up in the wash, random drawers, under the sofa. On my way to a speaking engagement, I discovered I didn't have a collar tab with me. I searched in my car in the church parking lot, wondering what to do. I figured out that my business card, carefully folded, would do in a crisis. It's such a little thing — but it makes a big difference.

06 FRIDAY OCTOBER 06

Compass Points North

"Buddy" just got back from work in Alaska. Tonight at Dravus Street, he spoke the truth to another patron.

"When I was sixth grade, I read everything, and decided to read the Bible. My family didn't have any church connection or anything.

"Then in seventh grade I got it." He points to his heart. "Since then I know I am all right. It's like when I'm on the boat; I know I get off course, but I check my compass, pointing me north. I always got that compass, getting me back on course."

06 SUNDAY NOVEMBER 19

Wedding Fun

Just so you know it's not all homeless and bar ministry, I did a wedding on Orcas Island in the San Juan Islands this weekend.

The bride was marrying a Lebanese guy.

After the rehearsal at the church, we had to get back to Shaw Island, a short channel hop away, for the rehearsal dinner and the various homes where guests were lodged.

Well, it was going to take two trips. It would be quicker just to put a few extra people aboard, and it didn't seem too bad. It was a familiar passage to our skipper, about a fifteen-minute trip one way.

So we all crammed into our craft — eleven adults, three kids. Did I mention the groom couldn't swim? And that I sat in the aft with a forty-pound box of baklava on my lap?

About two-thirds of the way home, Homeland Security forces accosted us from out of nowhere in the pitch black. We were ordered to stay on the dock, had to give our personal information, explain what we were doing and why. The two Lebanese guys with us had to produce ID and talk with the officers. It was pretty scary; funny; worrisome.

What will happen? We don't know. The boat was overloaded, there were not enough flotation devices for the number of people, and evidently the owner had not renewed his boat registration for the year (this same boat has been delivering mail in the islands for a while). We're praying for a warning for the skipper; lesson has been learned without a fine, I would think.

Meanwhile I was unsuccessful in convincing the Coast Guard that baklava is a flotation device.

2007

07 WEDNESDAY MAY 30

Homeless Shelter Flood

Emergency call came at the crack of 9:00 a.m. from the substitute shelter manager.

"There's been some sort of disaster, the toilet overflowed, the workers cleaned it up, but there's still water on the carpet."

Oh, the humanity.

Then the church janitor reported, "Toilet paper in the sanctuary!"

Good grief. How bad was the damage, and what the heck's going on.

"Sink's plugged too."

Wow, sounds serious.

We go running over to see what is going on. By now it turns out to be simply a plugged toi-toi, easily plunged out, and hair in the P-trap.

No mention of the TP in the sanctuary. I'm imagining some old lady spilling her purse out to find a bit of Kleenex to dab at the eyes after an especially moving choir number?

Just another chapter in my book about janitors who don't know what a toilet auger is.

07 MONDAY JULY 02

Cross Connections

I met Bob sleeping in his VW Bug about twenty years ago. (He keeps track, I don't.)

Bob has come and gone and come and gone, but appears to have put a good run together this time.

In fact, he got to travel with North Creek Presbyterian to do Katrina relief a few months ago. Formerly homeless guy, doing front-porch repairs and drywall finishing. How cool is that?

07 TUESDAY OCTOBER 09

The Song

There is music
That runs through me
Sometimes pizzicato
Sometime adagio
Sometimes harmonic
And then dissonant.

How about you?

Do you feel the stars
Vibrating
To a sweeping unheard symphony
Resonating inside and out?
Do you feel the thump
Of bass
As God's low-rider,
Windows down,
Makes life jump for joy?

So why do you hear
That same tune
And tap your toe
In synch with me,
And the others
I love
Do not?

I sing alone,
But not alone at all.
I sing with you
Wherever we find ourselves
Under the same
Shimmering sun
Vibrating stars.

2008

08 FRIDAY JANUARY 11

Blast From the Past

Took three college students around last night. We were drowning in pastries, so we shared with Tent City 3 and with St. Martin de Porres shelter. Took coffee to Bread of Life.

Then went to the old neighborhood, parking in front of 91 Wall Street, Nightwatch location from 1994 to 1997.

It was so quiet and weird.

There wasn't a single homeless person around anywhere. The block of the Millionaire Club was deserted. First Avenue was quiet except for the required intense conversation between a twenty-seven-year-old office worker and her next boyfriend as they had a smoke outside the organic restaurant.

I stood in the alley where so many homeless guys have pissed, and told my impressionable companions this story:

> Midafternoon, on a hot day in the summer, I come into the alley to dump the trash. Some guy is sleeping right in the middle of the alley, totally exposed to the sun and God and the garbage trucks that rumbled by constantly.
>
> I lean over him. "Hey, buddy! Are you okay?"
>
> He feebly lifts his head. "Yeah, it's all good."
>
> But I could see the chewing gum from the alley stuck to the back of his head. Not good.

08 TUESDAY JANUARY 08

What Are the Chances?

Last week I got a call from one of our Nightwatch tenants living in the senior apartments. He's been in the hospital and now a nursing home in the north end.

"There's someone here that wants to say hi," he tells me.

Then a strange voice. "Bet you can't guess who this is!"

You're right.

"It's your old friend, Loser."

My mouth fell open. Loser (not his real name, duh, but the one he went by when I knew him twelve years ago).

Loser slept in his van outside Nightwatch when we were in another neighborhood. He helped out around the place, and helped himself a tad too. Think "biker dude." He has a toad sticker about ten inches on the front seat of his van. No one messes with him. He gets his blankets from homeless people in the morning for a buck. Somehow he survives.

Next thing I knew, Loser was the manager of a downtown apartment building. He actually helped me get Herschel off the street after we got the social security stuff taken care of.

Every few months we'd check in with each other. Okay, maybe once, twice a year. You know how it goes. I thought he left town. Last time I checked, his replacement at the apartment building didn't know what happened to him.

Anyway, remember the senior tenant — John — who called me? They're assigned to the same nursing home room in the north end. John and Loser, side by side. The mind reels. What are the chances? Both are hanging on to life, for now.

08 TUESDAY FEBRUARY 19

Funny Story

Okay, read below, and you'll figure out why this old story popped in my mind:

> Guys come in all the time without any ID; we don't even ask for it because it just makes an artificial hurdle for someone wanting help. ID gets lost and stolen, and I've seen fake ID that someone got for $40, anyway. We aren't the police.
>
> So we found some new guy a place to go — he signed in, and was waiting. Dispatch worker is announcing, "Fred Smith, Fred Smith," and no one is moving. "Person going by the name of Fred Smith!" Finally, that gets someone going. We make another announcement:
>
> "Guys, if you gave us a fake name, please remember which fake name you used, it will help us a ton. Thank you."
>
> The rest of the gang had a nice chuckle.

08 SATURDAY MARCH 01

Popcorn, Anyone?

My second month on the job, about May 1994, one of our homeless clients snapped. Without provocation he started breaking out plate glass windows in our rented space. Boom, boom, boom, broken glass all over — and the forty or fifty homeless men and women on the sidewalk were practically shaking, they were so keyed up from this random display. I came running outside in time to see the fourth window go, and could feel the tension in the air. This took place just before we opened for the night, which was 10:00 p.m. at that time.

I turned to the folks in line outside and said, "If any of the rest of you are going to put on a show, I want you to call me out of the office so I won't miss it."

Without missing a beat, one of the homeless guys said, "If there's going to be a double feature, you've gotta provide popcorn."

Laughter filled the night air, the tension was broken, and we went on to have a great night.

The amazing thing — the next night, some unknowing donor came around with about forty gallons of popcorn, ready to serve.

I have to throw these stories up on the blog or I'll forget them, you know?

2009

09 THURSDAY JANUARY 08

Christmas 2001

Fumbling around for a notebook — a new brain for a new year — I ran across a "vintage" Christmas story from 2001. Humor me.

I was asked to speak to a group of inner city kids about Christmas.

These kids were from Yesler Terrace, Seattle Emergency Housing Services, Operation Nightwatch.

More specifically — they were from Somalia,
Ethiopia, Vietnam, Cambodia, and the other side of the tracks.

A tough crowd. Many cultures, languages, traditions. Life had been tough for these families, and I was nervous. What did they know about Christmas? What would interest them?

I decided to get them talking.

"Tell me what you know about Christmas, about Jesus' birth. Use one word."

Hands went up. Words were written down.

Manger
Straw
Animals
Donkey (Here, every possible farm animal is added.)

"How about something besides animals?" I suggest.

A brief pause:

Star
Wise men
Angels

Mary
Joseph
Shepherds

(Egad, these kids know the whole story, what can I add?)

There was a lull. One young boy raised this hand for the first time.

"Trouble"

Yes, Jesus' birth was all about trouble: taxes, untimely pregnancy, homelessness, political uncertainty, religious longing, life itself.

Suddenly we all got it. Everyone has trouble — at school, in the city, the world. Trouble is everywhere.

Nice to know we're not alone. Jesus had trouble too.

09 FRIDAY JANUARY 09

No Room

Two items this week.

First, I got a friendly call from a local property manager.

Homeless people have been sleeping under a group of eight cottages in the neighborhood. Ben and I went to check things out.

These houses are vacant. Five of the eight were wide open to the world. No fencing, not even a door on the crawl space. Easy access, with mattresses. I alerted the manager to the impossibility of keeping homeless people out without at least securing the property. The next day, nothing had changed.

Second, last night we turned away seventeen men because all the severe weather shelters were closed. It was 37 degrees. Those seventeen guys got a blanket from us, and our best wishes for a good night sleep.

Tent City costs about $1.75 per person per night. A new overnight men's shelter would cost about $10 per person per night, assuming you could get some church to underwrite the space and utilities.

Those seventeen guys all wanted inside. What should we do?

09 TUESDAY JANUARY 13

Great Smile

My buddy stops me on the street. He has about six teeth left in his mouth, and they're ready to tip over.

"Think anybody can help me with these?" he asks, and shows me how loose the survivors are. I wince. Couldn't help it.

"I'd really like implants," he goes on. Hmmm. No one is going to spring for those. What about dentures?

"Tell the truth. I'm just paranoid enough to think they're going to take my teeth out, polish them up, and sell them to someone else." Paranoid is right. The tooth fairy can only take so much.

I suggested he get someone to pop him one, then have Harborview do the extractions. My friend demurred. We had a good laugh, he gave me permission to tell the story.

09 FRIDAY JANUARY 23

Tent City 3

Tent City 3 is located in Shoreline, about a mile from where I grew up. Tonight I followed my nose to the old neighborhood in the Edmonds/Woodway area after delivering socks. Just a little detour.

It's strange — driving past a house where a friend lived thirty years ago, and still feeling so connected to the place. I smiled, knowing that people I know probably drive past my old home in that neighborhood.

Do homeless people have these feelings, this sense of place? Absolutely!

I had this discussion with homeless friends in Belltown many years ago. Some had been kicked out of shelters for their bad behavior — too crazy or too high to sleep on a floor with other people. Yet they still malinger in the neighborhood. They feel safe with the familiar, even if that means familiar with a particular block, an alley, or a temporary squat.

Human beings are wired for "home-ness" whether they have an actual residence or not. It explains "Paul" living under Interstate 5 in the same location for over ten years. Workers come and clean things out, and a week later he's back, rebuilding. Always a touch of style too — salvaged carpet, the odd chair; not a slacker with the garbage heap nearby, Paul packs it out.

09 THURSDAY JANUARY 29

My Fifteenth Count

Counting homeless people was part of my job when I arrived at Operation Nightwatch in 1994. I'd round up a pair of homeless guys, send them out, coordinating the areas with the police department, and type up a two-page report for someone in the City of Seattle. The whole deal cost about $300, not counting my time.

I got this brainstorm — use volunteers to do the count and do it all in one night. That was 1996. We had twelve volunteers that first year, and we covered all of downtown Seattle starting at midnight. Everyone agreed it was too early.

The next year we lined the count up with the Seattle King County Coalition on Homelessness Shelter Survey, to get a snapshot of who is homeless in King County.

We were discovered by local media, the number of volunteers mushroomed, the area of the count grew.

The great thing that we fell into was hosting a breakfast after we were done counting. Counters took over a local cafe, I chalked the whole expense up to PR, and the elected officials jumped on the band wagon. I think they've all taken a turn at counting at some point.

Last year was amazing, as people all over King County are involved in this tremendous coordinated effort.

Last year we found 2,631 homeless people. What about this year? Tonight at 2:00 a.m. the fun begins.

09 SATURDAY FEBRUARY 14

Benedictus

I enjoy the incantations
Of the mentally ill,
Who pray for me
In curious languages
Known only by God.

And I am buoyed by
the charismatic cadences
Of sixth grade Four Square children
Praying "Lord God, Lord God" while pressing down
Small hands upon my head and shoulders.
How they pushed! Or, was I simply weary?

But today, a different blessing was bestowed:
Truck Driver Benediction
He looked me in the eye and shook my hand
Having faithfully delivered 3,000 homeless blankets
Compliments of the Defense Department.
"You're doing the Lord's work" he growled
With A Voice,
Created by Jack Daniels
And the strain of being heard
Over a twin-cam 96B Fatboy Harley.

"You're doing the Lord's work."
It made the rest of my twenty-hour work day
much lighter.
And that WAS a blessing.

09 MONDAY FEBRUARY 23

A Stop in Pueblo

Here's a story:

> In 1997 I was fortunate enough to help my friend Herschel get off the street. The first thing he did: had me write a letter to Wayside Cross Mission in Pueblo. Herschel wanted me to thank them for helping him, many years ago.
>
> For years, Herschel faithfully helped Operation Nightwatch in ways not noticed by many people. He was our gatekeeper; passing out numbered tickets so homeless guys didn't have to stand in line; mopped the floor; and later, when he moved into our apartment building, he picked up litter in the neighborhood, to keep us good with neighbors.
>
> Herschel was a man of few words. He could barely read or write. He'd get excited and tell me things like "Saw a '57 Chevy." When he had a problem, and I couldn't understand him he would get mad. "F—ing B—S—" he would say, clear as a bell.
>
> But despite the occasional blue language, he was a man at peace with the world. He knew his terminal disease could mean a miserable end. But his faith was an inspiration to me — and still is. Not very conventional, not churchy, but solid, real, meaningful, gritty stuff.
>
> So, I am on vacation this week, traveling from Albuquerque to Denver. I had to pull off in Pueblo and find the "Wayside Cross Mission" and tell them the story of Herschel's life. And to thank them again for what they did for Herschel.
>
> And for me.

09 FRIDAY MARCH 06

Train Wreck

First stop, Nickelsville, now located at Bryn Mawr United Methodist, near Renton. Not close, but, oh, well. Kudos to the church for hosting for three months.

Stopped at the usual places, nice conversation. Encouraged Da Nang to make up with his buddy. He said he would.

Then, on the way back to HQ I saw an old friend, struggling with drug issues. It's 11:30 at night, she's headed downtown. I pull a three-lane U-Turn and roll down the window. "You okay?" I ask her.

I know the answer, but I wanted to hear what she said.

"I'm just going downtown to meet my boyfriend." She's lying, lying, lying. She's going to make a connection.

She knows I know she's lying.

It's like watching a train wreck in slow motion. Just gotta stand back and let it happen. It's too late to wave lanterns or throw switches.

I'm going to bed, sick to my stomach.

09 WEDNESDAY MARCH 25

Passing of a Friend

My friend June passed away today. I'm sad.

In the mid-1970s, she decided the young adults at our local church had enough Sunday school. It was time go into action. So they organized "church" at Branch Villa Nursing Home in Seattle's Central District. Every Sunday morning, 9:00 a.m., instead of sitting around eating Danishes and arguing some esoteric doctrine, we gathered thirty residents and sang old-fashioned gospel songs with guitars, and sometimes with the piano stylings of a resident, Alta. One old vaudevillian would rise and sing solo. "Church in the Wildwood" might morph into "Pistol Packin' Mama." I stuck with it for ten years, every week. Others continued even longer, all started by June.

One old Skid Road denizen was released back into a flea-bag hotel. June found out where he was, and we took him a birthday cake. It was crazy fun. The guy was 70 and never saw anything like it. We passed out cake to everyone coming through the lobby.

Long before I had any sense of my life's work, June would tell me, "Rick, you're on," and I would have to get up in front of these old people and bring some word of encouragement. I might go on for four minutes, but that was pushing it.

Dang it. Death is no good.

09 THURSDAY MARCH 26

Twenty Men. Who Cares?

Tonight we told twenty guys that there's no shelter in the entire city of Seattle. "Here's your blanket, good luck. God bless."

If you've never done that, it is a sickening feeling.

Next week fifty more homeless guys will be turned out of the King County Administration building shelter. Forty women will be pushed out from Angeline's women's shelter. It's horrible.

Many of my friends would say, "The city of Seattle should do something." I say, forget the city of Seattle. YOU should do something.

If your congregation isn't providing space and volunteers for homeless people, SHAME on YOU. If you have resources, time, space, willingness — let's talk.

I would invite the policy-makers who decided April was an acceptable month for shelter closures to spend a few nights sleeping in their back yard with a blanket.

Why are we heating city hall when our citizens are sleeping outside?

09 MONDAY MARCH 30

Sullivan's Travels and April's Sadness

There is a scene in the 1941 Preston Sturges movie *Sullivan's Travels* that absolutely killed me this weekend. The male lead wakes up in a shelter without his shoes.

It's a stereotype. (There are a ton in this movie). But the thing they got right: Stuff happens when you're homeless, shelter or not. Your day-labor job ruins your only set of clothes. You set your bag down, turn around, and it's gone. You drop quarters in a phone and get a wrong number. Your friend takes off with the money for the deposit, you sprain an ankle, and on and on.

Now April is almost here. Surprise! More fun. April 1, a shelter closes for forty women (apparently it's mild enough, we don't have to be concerned about these forty women now facing being outside at night). There are fifty men facing the same fate when they close the shelter at the King County Administration building.

This winter-shelter stuff has been a problem the entire fifteen years I've been here. Can't we figure something out?

09 FRIDAY APRIL 03

Slow Night on the Street

I humbly offer a poem from last April in lieu of homeless currents.

Tonight, April 2008

Tonight I hugged a hooker,
And held the hand of an addict
Who assured me that everything
Was just fine;
Yet he was looking
over my shoulder
the whole time.
Tonight I breathed a prayer of blessing
In a place that smelled like beer
And piss.
Tonight I shook hands with a homeless friend
And talked baseball
Instead of asking
Why he won't deal with
The cancer he knows
is killing him.
Tonight I listened to a carefully coiffed drunk
With lustrous skin and perfect nails
Tell me how generous she is
(to a fault)
and I wondered how much she spent
on the gold leather coat,
the face lift, the teeth,
the boobs, hidden, lurking.
Tonight I talked to workers
Who served up food and shelter for 200

But had to send away twenty-three men
And six women
Into the rainy night
With nothing but a thin wool blanket.
Tonight I will have to dream some impossible dream
on behalf of twenty-nine miserable phantoms.
God help us all.

09 WEDNESDAY APRIL 08

More Homeless Seniors ...

How can you survive on $700 a month from Social Security?

Some old folks are sleeping in their cars.

Operation Nightwatch has twenty-four units for seniors, shared bath and community kitchen. Furnished room, with late night dinner thrown in for $250 a month. Must be 62+. It's amazing how many people can only afford that much rent.

I get the feeling we're about to see a huge shift in demographics in our homeless population.

The one comment, though, that I found interesting. One of the interviewees wouldn't give his name: "I don't want my kids to know I'm homeless."

Something haywire there.

The guy pictured here worked for ten years as a dishwasher before retiring in our building. Not sure where he would have ended up otherwise ...

09 MONDAY APRIL 20

Uncertainty

Life is uncertain.

We try to insulate ourselves from that uncertainty. But in the end, we all end up as compost.

So, what really matters?

Do you think all the junk in the garage is going to matter to anyone after you're gone? They're going to have a rummage sale, and what's left over will go to Goodwill, and whatever survives that will end up as land-fill. Are you sure you want to waste your life accumulating all that "stuff"?

My crisis this week is to help a family with four children find affordable housing when they have a family income of about $1,000 a month. Nice people. Just poor. A combination of bad breaks, poor health, and lousy job skills have led to this crisis. But they are so dang adorable.

Isn't there someone out there with an answer for me?

Would you be willing to take a chance?

09 SUNDAY APRIL 26

Earth Sunday

It's Earth Sunday.
Mists rise, primordial
A crow questions
the goodness
of a God
who requires such
hard work and suffering
while pulling out
Dick's fries
from the bag
at my bus stop.

09 TUESDAY MAY 05

The Drinker's Bargain

The booze hound says, "I'm okay, at least I'm not homeless."

The homeless boozer says, "I'm homeless and I drink, get over it. At least I'm not a junkie."

The junkie says, "It's organic. As soon as I get a place, I'll kick it. At least I'm not some old boozer."

It just goes round and round like that. As long as you can see someone else worse off, then you are okay.

I've seen serious alcoholics pulling down six figures. They have no pity for the homeless alcoholic, other than flipping a pan-handler a buck. When they feel like it.

Being self-absorbed and self-serving cuts across income, class, education, political opinion, orientation, and classification. What do you think?

09 THURSDAY MAY 28

little things matter …

From Robin, in the Nightwatch office:

> Almost every morning now when I get to work, "Chuck" is out front talking to the crossing guard. This morning (as usual) Chuck starts talking to me, asking me if I'm "working hard," etc.

[Chuck has a repertoire: "Keeping out of trouble?" "Working hard?" "Keeping busy?" Pretty much one of these three, every time he sees you.]

> Chuck mentions that his alarm clock didn't go off for some reason this morning. I asked him if he missed an appointment or something important. He says, "No, I set it so I get up in time to talk to the crossing guard."

[The crossing guard keeps track of the kids on the way to Gatzert Elementary. He's a retired sheriff's deputy, on duty before and after school at Fourteenth and Main.]

> It made me realize that little things in life make all the difference. Having a nice crossing guard makes Chuck want to get up and out of bed every morning. Just wanted to pass that story along, it just made me smile.

[Thanks, Robin]

09 WEDNESDAY JUNE 03

So Long, Bill

Bill went in the hospital two weeks ago. He thought it might be pneumonia.

Turned out to be something worse.

Last Wednesday he let it be known he wanted to be baptized. Thursday I talked with him about it.

Friday I went back. He confirmed his wish. So I baptized him while he lay in bed at Veteran's Hospital.

Bill liked being baptized. He smiled and said, "It's so easy!"

Very easy.

The next day I got a call from a neighbor. Bill was dead. Having made his peace, he simply let go.

09 TUESDAY JUNE 09

Forty Years

1969. The Seattle Pilots were playing their first and only year of major league baseball at Sick's Stadium. "Here Comes the Brides" was playing on television. (Bobby Sherman!) The tallest building downtown was the Smith Tower until the SeaFirst Building was completed later in the year.

1969 was the year that Rev. Norm Riggins put on a clerical collar and went out on the street at night for the first time with Operation Nightwatch.

Octogenarians usually take life easy. But ever since retirement, Norm and his wife, Bonnie, have volunteered their time. He still has been going to bars to greet patrons and bartenders; she distributes socks and hygiene supplies to homeless people two nights a month.

It gives meaning to life, to care for folks. But now Norm is having trouble. He's a little unsteady on his feet. But I won't count him out. He will fight it. The passion and drive are still there. It's just ... well, let's face it. The flesh is weak.

Forty years is a long time to stick with something.

09 MONDAY JUNE 15

What I'm Working On

Friday night, it's about a six-minute drive to Operation Nightwatch from one of the most fabulous houses in the region, bar none. Beautiful house, filled with beautiful women writing checks to support homeless sisters at Operation Nightwatch. They gave more than $20,000 in two nights.

Meanwhile outside Nightwatch, it's 9:00 p.m. and homeless people have lined up to get a decent meal and a place to go for the night. It's an interesting transition.

I'm greeting people and shaking hands and answering questions.

Some young guy says, "If I'm already a believer, what's the next thing I should be working on?"

Learn how to love people. That's what I told him, and he told me he thought that was a good answer.

09 FRIDAY JULY 03

Medical Crisis?

It was well after midnight in Pioneer Square, downtown Seattle.

I'm walking the Nightwatch beat in my clerical collar. At the corner of First and Yesler, I see a homeless guy on his back, flopping around like a fish in the bottom of a boat.

Now, having worked for a few years in a health care setting, I've seen lots of people having seizures. This guy looked like he was having a tonic-clonic episode.

I lean over him. "Hey, buddy! Buddy! You all right?"

Now, if he WAS having a seizure, he's not going to speak to me, so I'm not sure what I thought. His eyes were closed and by this time he's jerking, jerking, jerking.

He opens one eye and looks at me, hovering over him, worried.

"I'm ... just ... working ... on ... my ... abs."

Alrighty then ... on to the next crisis.

09 FRIDAY JULY 10

Awful Responsibility

Operation Nightwatch got a check with this note: “Rick — no return envelope, so am sending $10 again. Can afford to — am now getting $16 food stamps. Thanks for your prayers.”

Imagine the awful sense of responsibility that is mine, in spending that $10 to take care of homeless people.

09 FRIDAY JULY 31

A Shared Sadness

Thursday night, the heat broke. Better
my heart. It's hardness was sadly
revealed to me, too late to do much about it.

"How's your day?"
I innocently asked
a young man,
squatting along Broadway.

His pup lay beside him, dispirited.
Too tired, too hot. No wag left.
He barely lifted his head to acknowledge me.

The weary dog's owner thought about his day.

"They pulled some girl out of the water
at Madison Park" was his answer.

His street companion was incredulous.
"No shit? You saw this?"

"Yep."

The brief sad tale hung there for a moment,
all of us keeping silence.

I mumbled some
lame banal blessing,
and continued on my way.
"Pray for me will you?"
he shouts down the sidewalk.

So tonight I will pray.

I will pray for a young man,
witness to one great sadness
after another in his short life.

And I will pray for myself,
for eyes to see
at once,
instead of waking up
to a lost moment
a day later.

09 FRIDAY AUGUST 07

Highs and Lows

How could one night swing around so wildly?

Instead of our usual haunts, we met up with a former client "Will," now sober, and had ninety minutes of conversation in a coffee shop in Ballard (the new Belltown, I'm thinking).

It always takes me a minute to realize: "This is the same guy," because he was the worst toxic drunk I have ever known. And he's been alcohol-free nine years. No setbacks.

From this high, we stopped by Harborview — where an extended family member, "Maggy," is in the intensive care unit, having suffered a stroke. She's one of those people who always had a smile going. There are some tough choices coming in the next few hours. Wisdom and the Comforting Presence needed.

As we left Harborview, we encountered a hospital patient, outside for a smoke. Pretty scraped up, in a neck brace, "Dee" gave us a wild story — in prison eighteen of the past twenty-one years, he's decided to become a minister. Or a comedian. His stream-of-consciousness "screenplay" had hyper-religious overtones and crude prison references.

But through the mania and brokenness, there was something lovable and lovely about the guy, sitting there in the dark, nearly midnight, dressed in hospital garb and neck brace.

We said good-bye, and a half block away, he called out to us.

"I know it's kind of weird in our culture and all ...," his voice trailed off. "Can I have a hug?"

I watched as he hugged Father Kim, and then he bent down to hug me, and I could only think, "This is the best job in the entire world," because it was so thoroughly satisfying. Because of Will, I know the dead come to life. Because of that, I know Maggy will smile again, somewhere. And I know that problems can't be solved with a hug, but it sure doesn't hurt.

09 THURSDAY SEPTEMBER 10

On the Edge

Like our clients, Nightwatch teeters on the edge.

Their chaos becomes our chaos, their challenges are our challenges. Today someone asked about our "strategic plan." My answer would be "One Day at a Time."

So much needs to be done. There are 2,800 human beings sleeping outside tonight, in Seattle/King County. On any given night, over 8,300 people are homeless when you include shelters and transitional programs. I hear talk about building new apartments as a solution to homelessness. The cost of $225,000 per unit seems as crazy as the client who was sure that his brain was being controlled by satellites, and showed me a website to prove it.

Tonight after visiting two homeless encampments to deliver pastries, and stopping in two neighborhood pubs, Pastor Dave and I looked at each other and said, "What the heck did we get done tonight?"

On the way back to our Shelter Dispatch Center, we stopped by a Nightwatch shelter. Seventy-five guys were sprawled out on mats in a big room, sleeping. This is what we do. Every night.

At 11:45 p.m. one last homeless woman walks out the door with food and a new pair of socks.

No drama. But it matters. Yep.

09 MONDAY SEPTEMBER 21

Preamble

It seems like a debate that will never end. What role does government have in caring for citizens?

> *"We the People of the United States, in Order to form a more perfect Union, establish Justice, insure domestic Tranquility, provide for the common defense, promote the general Welfare, and secure the Blessings of Liberty to ourselves and our Posterity, do ordain and establish this Constitution for the United States of America."*

For the knuckleheads who object to government intervention, how do you think government can "promote the general Welfare" by ignoring the desperate situation that many people find themselves in today? A nation of sharply divided "haves" and "have-nots" will not lead to domestic tranquility. Homelessness, health care, poverty are shared problems. There will only be shared solutions. Everyone must shoulder some responsibility.

09 MONDAY OCTOBER 26

Some Sort of Record?

Brother Dave and I parked the car in White Center, took about ten steps on the sidewalk, if that.

"HEYYY! Are you ministers?" a woman asked. "Would you pray for me?" Sure.

She starts yelling at her friends, loitering outside a tavern. "Come over here, you need prayer!" One guy joined us, she kept yelling. "We need all the prayer we can get, come on," but there were no more takers. So we held hands, the four of us, and asked for God's strength and grace and healing.

It had to be some sort of a record for Operation Nightwatch — ten seconds from parking the car to responding to someone on the street.

I'm gonna need a stopwatch from now on.

09 SATURDAY DECEMBER 19

A Christmas Story From Yesterday

Need a little Christmas cheer? Here's a story from someone out buying gloves as presents for our homeless friends at Operation Nightwatch:

> I am at Sears buying gloves (Costco was sold out). A man approaches me asking why I am buying so many gloves. I tell him they are for Nightwatch and he says "Oh, good, I will go there tonight. Someone stole my tent and I'm cold."
>
> I told him to pick out any gloves he wanted and I would get them for him on the spot. He couldn't believe it and started telling everyone that passed, "She is an angel; I found an angel." My young son wished him Merry Christmas. My other son helped count the gloves to make sure we had enough for ALL the homeless men.
>
> Thank you for inspiring the life lesson of helping others.
> — Kristie

2010

10 FRIDAY JANUARY 22

Almost Midnight

It's almost midnight. We're ready to tell nine guys that they're out of luck, no more shelter in the city of Seattle for them.

The phone rings. "How many guys you send us so far?" one of the shelter workers asks.

"Seventy-six."

That shelter has a stated capacity of seventy-five.

"How many guys are left?"

"Nine."

"Okay, go ahead and send them."

Whew. Let there be peace in this place, and peace on the streets.

10 THURSDAY AUGUST 26

Nothing Better

There is nothing better
than looking into the smiling face
of a no-longer-homeless person.

It doesn't matter
how bad the dental work,
the smile
leaves me smiling too —
every time.

Cathedral bells
cannot sound any more joyful
than the jingle of keys
in the pocket
of the newly housed.

10 THURSDAY OCTOBER 21

Am I My Brother's Keeper?

"Listen; your brother's blood is crying out from the ground" (Gen. 4:10).

It's 9:15 p.m. on a mild night in October. I'm out on the sidewalk chatting with homeless folks, trying to get knit hats on the bare heads of people waiting for food and shelter.

The line is peaceful, gentle kidding, conversational, and orderly. Except one guy. Everyone is watching him, as he paces back and forth in the parking strip, disconnected from people and reality.

Just about everything about the guy is off. He looks like he gave himself a haircut in a dark room. His stream-of-consciousness jabber is barely recognizable as English. He is restlessly running his hands up under his shirt as he paces.

There were a few muttered comments in line. "Whack job." The entire line of homeless people looked at him warily.

"Here's someone I need to talk to," I thought.

I positioned myself in front of the pacer, so he had to stop. "I'm Rick," I said, sticking out my hand.

Egad. His hand was huge, beefy, muscular. Somehow, in and through the stream-of-consciousness jabber, a conversation took place. He quieted down. The pacing slowed, stopped. The jabber morphed into stories, of working in Alaska, and living with a son, but not anymore.

In fact, I'm told, no shelter in town will let him stay any longer.
The conversation ends abruptly. He wanders off into the uncertain night.

It may be easy for you to shrug. "What concern is it of mine?" Sometimes turning away from a problem is as brutal as bludgeoning a younger brother to death.

The ground itself will give testimony to our failure to care.

10 FRIDAY NOVEMBER 19

What Do I Believe? Hmmmm

The scene: crowded bar after a UW Husky win.

"What do you believe?" My new friend on the stool next to me was looking at me, smiling, pretty tipsy, slightly apologetic. And waiting.

The question hung there for a moment. I thought about the Apostles' Creed, an ancient statement of faith. Not a very good answer, under the circumstances.

I thought about all the variables. Substitutionary atonement, amillenialism. Health care for all.

I decided to keep it simple: "I'm a Christian. A Methodist."

"Hey, me too," he slurred, satisfied.

2011

11 FRIDAY JANUARY 07

David's Got Me Covered

David could barely keep his eyes open. "Maybe just a little ... tipsy." So he said. Maybe.

We talked for a while, about nothing in particular. He likes his place in the shelter, after so many years sleeping outside.

"Are you okay?" he suddenly asked me.

"What do you mean?"

"You got a place tonight?"

"Oh, yeah. I'm good." I think about my warm bed, surrounded by various comforts.

"Because, if you needed a place, I'd find you a room or something," David assured me. "We have to take care of each other. We're all family here." He waved his arm around the TV room.

Indeed.

I've been talking to homeless people steadily for twenty-eight years now. As far as I can remember, this is the first time I was offered accommodations for the night. It was the sweetest moment ever.

11 THURSDAY JANUARY 13

Good Luck

It was just one of those

single odd moments in

a packrat-full garage night

of moments.

An old man in the homeless shelter

was describing in great joy

the sensation of gaffing

a seventy-three pound

king salmon,
back in the day, before

everything

else

got away

from him.

We all murmured

quiet admiration

for his grand achievement, →

and then quietly thought

what might have brought him low.

And then

another patron

stood behind the Great Fisherman

and rubbed his buzzed-cut head
with great enthusiasm.

"For luck!" he proclaimed.

The room laughed.

"You got the wrong guy,"

the Great Fisherman exclaimed.

We laughed again. But we all felt the pain.

11 FRIDAY APRIL 15

Dubious Record

Last night, 205 desperate people came to Nightwatch for help. The final forty-five minutes were painful, handing out hats, talking about options, passing out blankets and bus tickets. There were twenty-eight men and women with no rudimentary shelter of any kind. Every shelter in Seattle was full.

The full range of human emotions were demonstrated. Rage, humor, compassion. (One guy took a blanket, then gave it away.) Sadness. Lots and lots of sadness.

April is the worst month to be homeless in Seattle. Surprised?

City Hall housed seventy-five guys all winter; the Frye Apartment lobby was temporary home to twenty-five to thirty women, King County Admin building hosted fifty men, Angeline's winter shelter housed forty women. There was a winter shelter in Redmond for forty people. These all were closed April 1. One night, you're on a mat in a warm place, and then next night, good luck. April weather.

One final image from our Thursday night of pathos. An older woman, pushing her walker, dragging a travel bag and her little dog on a leash, was one of those going without shelter. She quietly asked to have us call an ambulance. "Where would you like to go?" we asked.

"Virginia Mason."

I gave her and the dog a lift to the ER. Hopefully the belligerent drunk at the entrance would keep the security people busy enough, they won't notice her sleeping in a chair in the waiting room.

It's 12:15 a.m. Tonight is another night. God save us.

11 TUESDAY MAY 17

The Face of Homelessness

Danny was a worker. He lived in the doorway of Operation Nightwatch. The weekend he was supposed to return home to the Tri-Cities, he got a phone call. "Never mind. Dad died."

Every night Danny would help me by mopping the floor, and helping to get the last guy out the door after midnight. Then he would lay out his sleeping bag on some cardboard. Night after night after night.

I know that homeless people are seen as useless, lazy, addicted, mentally ill, throwaways. It's easy to think that way, if you don't know anyone personally. But I have found my un-housed friends to be charming, hard-working, weary, forthright, and generous. Yeah, they got problems. So do I. So do you.

Why does it have to be such a stinking hard time to figure out basic shelter?

This week Operation Nightwatch has been serving about 190 to 200 people every night. Sunday night we ended up sending twenty-seven people out into the rain with a Metro ride ticket and a blanket. Men and women.

Saturday night we got eight guys into Saint Mary's Catholic Church. As I was driving away, I wondered why it is so hard to find two volunteers to spend one night a month hosting eight homeless guys. Can you tell me why?

Just so you know. We deliver in case you want to start something at your church or synagogue.

11 WEDNESDAY JUNE 01

Take Eight

For the past month, St. Mary's Catholic Church in Seattle has been taking eight guys from Operation Nightwatch to sleep overnight.

Every week, the same eight guys are hauled up the hill to Saint Mary's. Two volunteers greet them. Mats are laid out, guys sit around chatting, reading, settling in. By 10:15 p.m. everyone — including the volunteers — are hunkered down.

I drove away last Saturday night wondering why more congregations couldn't do something like that. Once a week for a month, take eight guys. Find two volunteers.

Eight guys. Pick a night of the week. Try it for a month. Two volunteers. Coffee and a roll would be nice in the morning, but not required.

It would mean eight fewer guys sleeping outside. Think about it.

11 FRIDAY OCTOBER 07

The Intoxicated Evangelist

We stopped at a shelter — guys are watching TV. Suddenly a very drunk man sees me and shouts, "Read something from my Bible!" And then he lurches around the room, grabs a Bible sitting on the table. We take turns reading, me choosing something from Isaiah, which included a promise of fine aged wine in the coming good times. Probably not the best choice. He goes straight to Romans.

After several selections back and forth, he says to me, in a not-so-loud drunken whisper, "I graduated Catholic. I went to war. This is all I have left," patting his Book.

And that is a sermon. Cue the organ.

11 FRIDAY NOVEMBER 04

A Prayer for John

How can I pray for John, who hobbles from his wheelchair to the bed
In the shelter that is a poor substitute for a nursing home?
He was crushed by a car, body and spirit.
His bridges burned, John looks now, in half-hearted jest
For another bridge.
This one for jumping.
After 40-something years, there are no lifelong friends. No family to rally him,
No platoon members to save him, no co-workers to greet him,
no former neighbors or lodge brothers to slap him on the back and smile
Not a single sister, deacon, usher, or Sunday school teacher
From the store-front Missionary Baptist Church of his childhood
Who will weep with him and treasure his soul.
And now, in a random encounter, he grips my hand and asks for prayer.
I am a stranger.
How can I pray for John of the burned bridges and the broken body?
I sigh deeply, knowing.
His needs are mine too.
"Lord, grant us Wisdom to know Your will, and the strength to do that."
From these two things, come all the rest;
peace, joy, brothers, sisters, and greener pastures.

11 THURSDAY DECEMBER 15

Christmas?

I hate getting dressed up. I especially hate getting dressed up on a Saturday afternoon for live theater. It's so unnecessary. But my wife and mother both told me it was required. What could I do? I sat in the theater, wearing a suit and tie, on a Saturday afternoon in December. I was resentful and hating. Bah, humbug.

The play was called *The Best Christmas Pageant Ever*.

I'm watching the show and thinking about all the work I needed to get done. Grrrr. Stupid play.

At some point, a brat of a character named Gladys jumps out, in angel costume, and yells, "SHAZZAM! For unto you a child is born," and she pointed right at me.

It was like taking a punch to the gut. I was mugged by Christmas. It snuck up on me and laid me out. All my resentments and grumpiness drained away.

I have to pay attention this time of year, or I'll miss the point. How about you?

2012

12 WEDNESDAY MAY 30

Major Accomplishments

"What are the major accomplishments of the project," asks the bank, which we are humbly approaching for a grant.

The amount of money that we are asking for will pay for shelter, enough to keep our guys inside for about ten nights. They will be safe. They will get better rest than the guys forced to sleep outside. I'm having trouble coming up with "major accomplishments" of offering basic shelter every night.

Why are they in this position of being homeless anyway? They're working, but they can't afford a place to stay for the little bit of money that they earn. They're disabled, but the little bit of disability they get isn't enough to pay for a place to stay. They're damaged goods, so no employers will hire them.

I would like to ask the bank, "What major accomplishments have you had as a bank? We're keeping people alive who can't afford your mortgages, who have to survive on your minimum wages, who don't have enough to live on since you won't pay enough taxes, and love guns more than butter. What are you doing to change this mess?"

This will not help Nightwatch get a grant from a bank. But just writing it makes me feel a little better.

12 THURSDAY MAY 31

"Let the Person With Two Coats Give to Him Who Has None"

If people don't have a coat, it's their own darn fault. They need to get a job and earn their own coat.

Funding for coats is being cut.

You can maybe get a grant for a coat. Please limit your answers to 250 characters in length.

Describe the anticipated impact of this coat grant. How will these impacts be measured?

Describe how you will inform the community of the coat grant. Is there a media plan in place for this program?

Limit one coat per household.

How will the coat be used?

This community is determined to eliminate the need for coat-sharing in the next ten years. We want to end coat-lessness, not manage it. How will this grant for coats end the need for coat-sharing in the future?

Sigh.

12 FRIDAY AUGUST 03

Ministry of Popsicles

"The best thing," the homeless woman told us, "is when you are almost done eating, and you're licking the last bit of goodness, and you get to taste the stick ... You made my week."

Such ecstasy.

We distributed sixty creamsicles at Tent City 3 late last night. The love of God is quiescently frozen at times. So good.

12 FRIDAY SEPTEMBER 07

Out of Place

I remember training a new worker at Operation Nightwatch, about fifteen years ago. An elderly woman came in, looking for food and shelter. The new worker was incredulous. "She could be my grandmother!" he whispered to me. Yup.

Last night I remembered that moment again. I was out visiting various camps and shelters. A young lady and I struck up a conversation. I wasn't sure if she was a homeless person or new shelter staff. Bright, articulate, talking about her college degree, family situation, what it's like to be homeless. She looked out-of-place.

There are no typical homeless people really. People are people. The lack of access to everyday comforts takes a toll, and that might show. But whether a homeless person looks like "us" (whatever that means) or is rough around the edges, they're all loveable in their own way.

12 FRIDAY OCTOBER 12

Aunt Rhoda and the Homeless Guy

Everyone should have an Aunt Rhoda in their life. My Aunt Rhoda was unforgettable. She wore white gloves. She drank her tea in fancy cups, with little sips. She didn't put her elbows on the table.

When I was eighteen, Aunt Rhoda visited Seattle. She insisted I borrow her 1972 Mark IV Lincoln Continental Town Car for the evening. I had nowhere to go, so I loaded up eight or ten Seattle Pacific students (read "coeds") into the beast, and drove to Herfy's — a local fast-food burger joint that didn't see too many Mark IV's in the parking lot.

Aunt Rhoda was a character. She may have been in the 1 percent but she was our 1 percent and we didn't care. We loved her.

In due time Aunt Rhoda died. For twenty-four years now I have been holding on to her dictionary. It looks as new as ever, though I am certain that Aunt Rhoda kept it better dusted than I ever did. This week, the dictionary along with three other boxes of books were loaded into my car, destined for Goodwill.

They were in the back of my car when I was loading blankets for homeless sleepers downtown. Manager Ben says, "What are those?" Books I'm getting rid of. "Donate them to the Nightwatch book rack," Ben tells me.

So I'm loading up the homeless-guy bookshelf at Nightwatch. Usually it's a bunch of Zane Gray westerns or Agatha Christie murder mysteries. Look, doesn't Aunt Rhoda's dictionary fit nice there?

I laughed. Aunt Rhoda's dictionary at Nightwatch. How funny. Even better, I can imagine her laughing at the absurdity of it too.

We spend a lifetime accumulating all this stuff. But whether we are an Aunt Rhoda, a homeless guy, or somewhere in between, we are all going to end up not needing that stuff anymore. It's so much better giving it away now, sharing what we have for the benefit of all. All that junk is too heavy to lug it around anyway.

Travel light.

2013

13 WEDNESDAY JANUARY 16

Jesus and the Spa Treatment

Last Sunday night I spoke at a retirement center near here. One of the seniors quoted Jesus "The poor you will always have with you ...," and asked if it doesn't all seem a little pointless, helping poor and homeless folks.

I've had the question before. In the gospel, Jesus was lounging at Lazarus' house, apres-Laz's resurrection. Sister Mary comes in and pours a pint of very expensive oil over Jesus' feet and wipes them with her hair. For this loving act, she is chastised by Judas. Then Jesus says, "The poor you will always have with you, but you will not always have me." He is quoting from Deuteronomy 15:

> *Give generously to (the poor) and do so without a grudging heart; then because of this the LORD your God will bless you in all your work and in everything you put your hand to. There will always be poor people in the land. Therefore I command you to be open handed toward your fellow Israelites who are poor and needy in your land.*

It's pretty much the opposite of how the verse is used by some.

13 MONDAY MARCH 25

Faith and Mental Illness

"Brad" is a sixty-five-year-old who suffers terribly from his mental illness. He has recurring and persistent delusions that someone is trying to kill him.

It's absolutely absurd, but it's as real to him as the page in front of you right now.

Imagine what it would be like if someone were REALLY trying to kill you. Your heart would pound, your palms would sweat, you would be on edge. Well, this is how Brad lives his life every moment of every day. He believes that a French actress, Audrey Tautou, is actively trying to kill him. It's as real as real can be, at least to Brad. And totally absurd.

Yesterday, Brad met with me for a simple quiet time of reading the lectionary readings for that Sunday. Various scripture passages are laid out over a three-year cycle, which follows the church calendar — Advent, Epiphany, Lent. This Sunday was Passion Sunday — the beginning of Holy Week for the Western church.

> These words from Psalm 31 especially struck home:
> *For I hear many whispering,*
> *"Terror on every side!"*
> *They conspire against me*
> *and plot to take my life.*
> *But I trust in you, LORD;*
> *I say, "You are my God."*
> *My times are in your hands ...*

Brad gave me a knowing glance, and afterward, remarked on it. "That passage in the Psalms really spoke to me." He was more calm.

Even in the midst of bad brain chemistry, I believe the knowledge that God is present, and brings relief to Brad. Our times are in his hands.

13 FRIDAY APRIL 19

Meditation on Delusion

Last night on the street, I had someone tell me a story. I can't tell you any of the details, just to preserve some shred of pastoral confidentiality. It was utterly delusional.

When I think about what I heard, I can only shake my head. Poor guy. It's not going to end well.

I've had many delusions shared with me through the years. Here are just a few:

"Satellites control my thoughts." The guy even directed me to a website where there was an X-ray of the device, which (he believed) was implanted in his head. Proof!

"I just (choose one) won a million dollars/inherited three million dollars/designed a new computer part worth a million dollars." Last time I checked, all three of those guys are either in a homeless shelter, or sleeping on a sympathetic person's sofa.

"That Swedish blonde I've been corresponding with online won't mind me being (pick one or both) twice her age/twice her weight."

"I'm just fine." This was said to me by someone lying fully prone on his back, in the middle of an alley on a hot day in downtown Seattle. When he lifted his head off the pavement to reassure me, I could see that the chewing gum in the alley had wound itself around his hair. Fine, indeed.

"I'm homeless because my old lady kicked me out. It has nothing to do with my drinking." So, maybe if you sober up, she'll let you come home?

One thing I've noticed: The delusions of others are always more ridiculous than our own.

13 MONDAY APRIL 29

I Worry About Dumb Things

A friend sent me a text. Her friend has cancer. He's getting treatment. Would I visit?

I was happy to go see this person in the hospital, despite knowing nothing about his situation. He's a friend of a friend. What else do I need to know?

At the hospital, I'm given thirty minutes free parking. After that, I have to pay. THAT's what I'm worried about. I get out of the car thinking "Thirty minutes. Go."

Negotiating the proper door to go through after hours, no problem. Facing a crowded emergency room, fine. Getting past the embattled nurse. Easy. Security guard? A snap. Up to the proper room. Done.

We had a pleasant exchange, me and the patient/friend. "Our friend sent me. I must obey!" This got a laugh out of him. He explained to his other visitors our connection: homeless-program-pastor-who-stops-off-at-a-bar. "The Sock Guy" he calls me. "I need all the help I can get," he tells me. So I pray for my sick friend, because doctors can only do so much and the Mystery that lies beneath their good work is precious, and life is a gift from the One who raises the dead.

As I leave, I'm laughing at myself for worrying about paying for the parking. I drive out, the attendant is gone, and the gate is up.

13 MONDAY AUGUST 19

Lauds and Compline

i.
I walk in the heavy morning air of mid-August,
suffocating, yet elated.
Despite my awkward old-age heaviness,
exhilaration exudes from the marrow.
A good Creator has, despite my contrariness,
granted a new day.
So I walk, in gratitude,
singing to myself the hymns of my childhood.
I conclude with the remembrance, long dormant,
of an obscure fourth verse. So satisfying!
Then, I detect a fellow walker,
emitting an indistinct sound from some device.
"How dare he infringe my worship with his din?"
Then, I draw closer, and the noise resolves
into Gospel.
Tempo, chords, and composition, are foreign
yet the same good Creator
is praised, with joy and power.
And so for a quarter mile, I lurk
within worshipful distance.
We meet by and by.
So sweet.
My new brother, Solomon.

ii.
Late that same night, world-weariness presses down the old preacher.
Yes, there is still joy, but the feet are sore and the bed beckons.
"Just a bit further. The time for resting is not yet."
In a dim shelter, residents fill my ear with stories

of logging, and methadone programs, and favorite authors.
Yes. It is as random as it sounds.
Then, bursting in,
a new, angry friend,
like a prophet, but all noise,
never resolving into Gospel.
Dramatic confusion born out of hurts
— personal and tribal —
he quotes myriad unrelated scriptures without understanding.
And yet, there is something loving and lovable
about a man who bears the burden of a daddy shot by drug dealers,
and the desire to make sense out of the inhumanity and cruelty
poured out on a race for generations.
I can do nothing about the slave trade. Nothing about the drug dealers.
Nothing about the hurt and pain he experiences daily.
Nothing but love.
I can hope that when the Morning comes,
and this long night is over,
John will be my brother too.

2014

14 MONDAY FEBRUARY 10

Hole in the Fence

There's a hole in the fence in my town.
It looks too small for a person to crawl through
but we do —
pushing hard to get through
like oversized
babies.
When we go through that
hole in the fence
we enter a world of despair.
Last night at midnight
we pressed corpulent flesh
through that hole
and entered into a dark world
under a highway.
Homeless people sleep here
wrapped up in cardboard, plastic, and blankets.
A community of sorrow and regret,
they clump together for safety
more than warmth.
Our blankets were received with thanksgiving
and amazement. It's 26 degrees.
My friend and I were quiet
until we squeezed back through the
hole in the fence.
What was there to say?
This is the world we live in,
where 700,000 people cram the streets
to celebrate civic pride
but not a single one
knows about the hole in the fence.

6 Feb 2014

I wrote this after crawling through a hole in the fence to take blankets to some guys who were camping out under a roadway in Seattle on a bitterly cold night — maybe in the low 20s. It was about midnight. My companion, Deacon Frank had never seen anything like that. So sad. This was one day after the massive Seahawks Super Bowl celebration parade. Never has Seattle been so packed with people, and none knew about the hole.

14 FRIDAY MARCH 14

Malachi Is Reborn

It's 10:00 p.m. I'm at a shelter, having just delivered the excess pizzas from Little Caesar to the residents. Some guy sees me, all excited: "I reborn today, I reborn today!" in heavily accented English.

To tell you the truth, I thought maybe he was reacting to my clerical collar, and had experienced some a transcendent spiritual moment, some movement of the Spirit. He shuffled through a clutch of papers.

"I reborn." He repeated. Then he pulls out a sacred document: "Certificate of Naturalization." His smile is lighting the room. Wowsers. Congratulations!

It has all come together for Malachi. He is now an American citizen, and a priest appears, bearing pizza in honor of this special day. With gestures, Malachi gives thanks to God above and to me, as though I had planned all this out, just for him. Five pizzas, deep-dish pepperoni, lowered from on high. Render unto Little Caesar's that which is Little Caesar's and render unto God that which is God's.

From Somalia to the United States. Malachi belongs with us now. Eat pizza. Be happy.

14 TUESDAY MAY 20

A Shadow

A wisp, a shadow, stood pawing through a garbage can at Third and James late last night. He muttered to himself and walked away.

"Hey, buddy. BUDDY." He looked at me with empty eyes. "You hungry? I got a pizza for you."

I opened the hatch on my car. The shadow's eyes grew wide, staring at thirty-seven pizzas, destined for other homeless friends. I picked up a deep-dish pizza box and handed it to him. For a moment he was coherent, substantial, alive. He thanked me, and turned away.

Human beings should not have to eat from garbage cans in our community.

When you give to Nightwatch, you reaffirm the dignity and worth of every human being who haunts our urban streets. You sustain them with food, offer them shelter. You grant hope and love to folks who have not experienced hope or love in a very long time, if at all.

14 FRIDAY MAY 23

Emergency

A homeless woman groans,
inching her wheelchair
toward nowhere in particular.
It's 11:18 at night.
I look at the Emergency Room workers.
They look at nobody,
afraid of the condemnation and hopelessness —
— the bitterness — brewing in that room of sufferers.
The woman groans some more, yet mildly.
breaking the concentration of the rest of us
who stare at workers not looking up.
Those gentle groans come from deep within.

The groaner knows.
There is no place for her.
She is not sick enough for a hospital
She is too alive for the morgue.
She is too needy to stay with friends
She is too unwell for a shelter.
There is no shelter.
There are no friends.
No hospital bed, no nurse, no doctor.
No tidy little apartment
where she could water a plant
drink tea and induce purring.
And so she groans.
She can do nothing else.

14 MONDAY JUNE 09

The Panhandler

There is a space
between the lines
between the words
where there is room
for the real story of a life
to be discovered,
tasted, smelled, handled.
**
That guy on the corner —
an aged drunk, using all guile to
extend his buzz —
was
quoted, with all eloquence
fifty years ago. Today,
I held the magazine
and read the quote
and heard it read
and shook my head.
**
There is an instant
between the days
between the moments
when there is time
for the real story of a life
to be discovered,
tasted, smelled, and handled.

14 FRIDAY JUNE 13

Legion

Last night at midnight
we looked into the face
of a homeless wretch —
a man, living in total subjugation
to his primal disordered brain.
With hurricane force
he spewed raw anger,
screaming irrationally at those
who want to help, but can't.
There is no shelter to contain him.
No options. In any program. Anywhere.
Until he throws a punch,
pulls a knife,
jumps out a window,

he is free to wander through the night.
His name is Legion. We have seen him before.
He is gathering strength.
God bless those shelter workers
who persevere
in the face of Belial.

14 MONDAY AUGUST 11

Fudgsicles

It was a single stroke of genius,
an oasis in a desert of a bungled day
when I decided
Fudgsicles
should be given to heat-afflicted homeless people.

Deacon Frank and I paraded around
a homeless camp,
no Pied Piper needed,
no out-of-tune tinny music on an endless loop
like the summertime daily attraction of my childhood.

Our homeless friends found us in all our abundance,
dishing out one here, two there,
and the numbers grew, another and another
and then the wave broke.
We stood around, finally,
talking survival, clutching our
thawing boxes,
happy homeless friends with
chocolate running down,
chocolaty lips smacking,
the delicate savoring
of the stick.

As we left, we offered the remains,
and found reluctant takers
one here, one there.
The last one offered is declined.
"I'm fudged out!"
and we laughed together. →

It is as it should be for all of us at times.
That abundance.
You may not have a roof over your head,
you may be overwhelmed with life
you may have a really crappy day,
but then
Fudgsicles.

14 TUESDAY SEPTEMBER 16

Step It Up

Hey, Preach. You for real? Listen to me, man.
I give good advice to everyone but myself,
Lord, don't I know.
I tell my friend what to do with his money,
Then throw mine away.
I need you to pray for me. Right now.
It's the right time. Use the right words. Pray.

— I pray for his wisdom and strength.
Amen. You know what? This shelter is fine.
They give you food, and clothes, and a place to sleep.
But they don't give you nothing for right here.

His bony finger jabs his chest. *Right here.*
— poking at his heart.
You guys are here on Thursday.
We love the pizzas and all,
but a man needs more than food.

Silently, he points to his heart again.
You gotta step it up. Once a week won't do.
Yeah. Step it up.

14 FRIDAY NOVEMBER 14

Walking Under the Interstate

> "Never depend upon institutions or government to solve any problem. All social movements are founded by, guided by, motivated and seen through by the passion of individuals."
>
> — Margaret Mead

> "Institutions do not serve persons; only persons serve persons."
>
> — Herb Dimock

Interstate 5 is not an institution. It is concrete, rebar, steel. It has no soul. Yet it may be the single biggest provider of shelter in King County. There is no human face for Interstate 5, just the cold, loud roar of machines, and tires thumping over expansion joints.

And beneath, from the trash, in passing, a spark. A stuffed toy, abandoned on the edge of a homeless camp — one of many camps in that dismal inhospitable place.

This toy asks us a question: Is Interstate 5 the best we can do for sheltering a human being who was at one time comforted by a stuffed bear?

Apparently so. We allow this to happen because we have closed up our hearts, our minds, our homes, our churches, our parking lots, our parks, our public buildings. Surely we will reap the whirlwind.

14 WEDNESDAY DECEMBER 17

A Light Shines in Charlotte

From Rev. Dr. Tom Kort, Sardis Presbyterian Church, Charlotte, North Carolina, December 24, 2000:

> I wonder if you know that something is going to happen tonight in this church that has never, ever happened before in the 210-year history of Sardis. This has never happened. Tonight, this Christmas Eve, for the first time ever in our goodly heritage, homeless neighbors will be sleeping at Sardis. They'll be here as part of "Room at the Inn." Think about it. "Room at the Inn." Bethlehem ... Jesus ... God's people ... It all starts to make sense, doesn't it?
>
> Let me tell you what happened a week ago when I came to "Room at the Inn" for the early 5:00 p.m. shift. That night we had nine homeless men, two homeless women, and a homeless child, age 2½. I hope I do not need to remind this congregation that the fastest growing population among the homeless are women and children. When I arrived, I noticed in the hallway a stack of books by a chair; and as I got closer I noticed that they were children's books. As I inquired about them, one of the members who had spent the night told me that the little boy, the one age 2½, had a very difficult time falling asleep. His father and the woman who was with him were dead tired, so they immediately fell asleep, but this little one just couldn't get his eyes to close. One of our deacons, a bright, young, single adult who spends all of her days uptown in the corporate world of Charlotte, took that little boy and held him on her lap, and in the warmth of her arms, she read children's stories until he fell asleep.
>
> The next morning, we had a hard time waking him up — 5:30 a.m. comes early to anyone. It comes early when you're →

only 2½. He cried, because he didn't want to get up. He wanted to stay where it was warm and safe; but we had to put him on the van with our other homeless neighbors, tears and all. His father came running back down the hallway. He'd forgotten something, and he saw me. Because they had asked me to say the grace at breakfast, he figured I was the preacher. He looked at me and said, "Would you do me a favor and tell all your people 'thank you'?" I said to him, "I never asked — what's the name of your little boy?"

He said to me, "His name is Emmanuel."

God with us. Now I do not know what you might make of that situation, but do you think that God was with us? Do you think it's possible that that is precisely and exactly what Jesus meant when he said, "What you have done for the least of these, you have done for me"? Do you think in all the significant things that happened that day in the city, in all the corporate buildings and oak-paneled offices, all the power-lunch meetings and all the million-dollar decisions that were made, do you think anyone took notice of a deacon holding a child? And if someone says, "Well, Tom, that's a nice story, but it's really not going to address the complexities of homelessness in this city," I'll say, "You're absolutely right." But don't you think that it's better for us to light one candle than just stand by and do nothing and curse the darkness?

And the story is told by John and it goes like this: "In Him was life, the light of the world." Never underestimate the power of God's light in this world.

14 MONDAY DECEMBER 29

Gift of Sarcasm

Under the "squeaky wheel" theory, one homeless guy persistently was distracting me as I was trying to coax a piece of junk formerly called a printer into some modicum of usefulness. It wasn't working, and a roomful of restless, tired, and cranky homeless people were waiting to be sent off to various shelters downtown. In their defense, any middle-class group of weary travelers would pose the same headaches, if not more so. After all, most homeless people have had all sense of privilege thrashed out of them along the way.

This night, the surging crowd and dark despair weighed everyone down. Even my usual chipper self was exasperated. The homeless dude in front of me was like a dripping faucet in the middle of a caffeinated nightmare.

Finally, I snapped. My own frustration and ire was directed at him. "OKAY," I said loudly. "I'M GOING TO STOP HELPING ALL THESE PEOPLE," (can you see me waving my arms around?) "AND JUST TAKE CARE OF YOU BECAUSE YOU ARE THE ONLY ONE WHO MATTERS HERE."

I'm pretty sure I didn't say any really bad words. I'm pretty sure I wanted to. But I do know that I was loud, and sarcastic, and hurtful. The gift of sarcasm is not God-given, pretty sure.

The squeaky wheel guy cut me down at the knees with one word.

He looked at me, turned up his nose, and said, "Hunh." That was it.

It was the most devastating "Hunh" ever used against me. "Hunh," meaning, "Here's the real you, Mr. Preacher Man. Sarcastic. Dismissive of us."

I love this job, because homeless people and homeless situations have a way of cutting through the complex fluff we build around ourselves to insulate and separate and categorize people. His body language and →

one word simply held up the mirror of reality, so I could see myself with distressing clarity for just an instant. It was devastating.

I got his full attention and apologized, loudly. The whole room needed to hear me eat crow, since they observed the offense. We parted friends.

Tonight, we launch a new chapter. Our eighty-bed shelter for men starts paying rent in a new location. This is the first time in seventeen years we've had to pay rent. Pray, volunteer, give.

Thank you.

seattlenightwatch.org

Made in the USA
San Bernardino, CA
26 February 2018